T0116517

THE CHARLOIS MANIFESTO

A practical philosophy for living an
abundant life

ROBERT A. CHARLOIS III

BALBOA.PRESS
A DIVISION OF HAY HOUSE

Balboa Press books may be ordered through booksellers or by contacting:

Balboa Press
A Division of Hay House
1663 Liberty Drive
Bloomington, IN 47403
www.balboapress.com
844-682-1282

Because of the dynamic nature of the Internet, any web addresses or links contained in this book may have changed since publication and may no longer be valid. The views expressed in this work are solely those of the author and do not necessarily reflect the views of the publisher, and the publisher hereby disclaims any responsibility for them.

The author of this book does not dispense medical advice or prescribe the use of any technique as a form of treatment for physical, emotional, or medical problems without the advice of a physician, either directly or indirectly. The intent of the author is only to offer information of a general nature to help you in your quest for emotional and spiritual well-being. In the event you use any of the information in this book for yourself, which is your constitutional right, the author and the publisher assume no responsibility for your actions.

Any people depicted in stock imagery provided by Getty Images are models, and such images are being used for illustrative purposes only. Certain stock imagery © Getty Images.

Scripture quotations marked NRSV are taken from the New Revised Standard Version of the Bible, Copyright © 1989, by the Division of Christian Education of the National Council of the Churches of Christ in the United States of America. Used by permission. All rights reserved. Website

Print information available on the last page.

ISBN: 979-8-7652-4495-1 (sc)
ISBN: 979-8-7652-4349-7 (e)

Library of Congress Control Number: 2023916231

Balboa Press rev. date: 08/23/2023

PREFACE

It is a cool spring evening, the moon partially obscured by a light cloud cover. The windows at the church across the street emitting a kaleidoscope of colors as they glow from the light from within. Just an hour before I left these halls, completing my report to the committee. All that was left was for them to rubber stamp my continued role as pastor.

One by one the cars left as the last of the members headed home. Now it is a waiting game for the call to arrive. I don't know why I'm anxious, this shouldn't be any different than the last four times we went through this process. This one seemed to go quite a bit longer than expected. Wait for the call. Everything is going to be fine.

Pastor Yancy, this is Margie. I wanted to call and give our report to you. We have decided to ask for a change in Pastoral Leadership. I'm sorry, but the decision was unanimous. I'll be sending the letter to the District Superintendent tomorrow. Have a good night.

I didn't know it then, but my life was about to change.

* * *

September 1st, 2021, a little over six and a half tumultuous years since that fateful evening and I'm typing the manuscript for my first book.

The first three years was a freefall through what Saint John of the Cross would call "A dark night of the soul." It was a period of confusion and uncertainty, where everything I had believed came into question. The rebel within me, suppressed most of my life, came out with a vengeance. But that was not nearly as hard as what was to come.

April 1st, 2018, began the journey through the Valley of the shadow of death. Six psychiatric hospitalizations, three medical hospitalizations, and homelessness, were all brought on by periods of psychosis, depression, and amnesia. Then finally, on November 12th of that year I was placed in Owingsville Manor, an assisted care facility in East Central Kentucky. The journey to wholeness began.

Recovery is slow and mine has been no different. But everything was in place for that recovery to take place. With the Manor taking care of my basic life needs, my family Doctor handling my basic health care, and Pathways Counseling services caring for my psychiatric concerns, recovery was almost certain.

The biggest aid in my recovery was the introspection that I began as part of my mental health therapy. Questions about my beliefs and values, discussion about who I wanted to be, and finally, where did I see it all heading? Part of the answer to that last question is in your hands.

*   *   *

I was speaking with my Pastor/Mentor/Friend/accountability partner Gordon Jones last night and we spoke of my book. That is not entirely accurate because it is not my book. Rather it is a compendium of thoughts and ideas that has spanned millenia

Robert M. Hutchins, editor of Encyclopaedia Britannica, wrote an essay titled, "The Great Conversation." In this essay he speaks of an ongoing dialog between the great thinkers of Western Civilization. It is in that vein that this book is being written.

I in no way am comparing myself to the great thinkers of history but I am attempting to gather the thoughts and words of those who are great. As I piece these together, adding my own effete words, I hope to continue this "Great Conversation." The theme, is an attempt at formulating "a practical philosophy for living an abundant life."

It is by gathering these items that I wish to make my case. Thesis; there are principles that we live by and roles we fill, if done for the right purpose, the betterment of mankind, will lead to an abundant life for all.

This idea is not new, mankind has been wrestling with this idea since the beginning of time. I believe we have a possible answer here and now as we examine the writings of the past and present.

I am gaining so much by exploring this subject and it is my hope and prayer that others will benefit from it as well.

* * *

I wish to thank all those who have made this book possible. Not only the great minds of history but also those who helped in other ways. Jamie Robinson, and Gordon Jones; my review team. It has been through their critique and suggestions that this is the quality I sought. My support team: Dinah Adamson, Tina Dorn, Tawnya Smith, Jamie Robinson, and Gordon Jones; they supported me for the whole of the journey. Terry Behymer, Jean Johnson, Dinah Adamson, and Gordon Jones; for contributing financially during the process. For technological support I need to recognize Reset Business Consulting and its founder, Maria Daniels. Then there are the countless others who have given encouraging words. No man works alone but is surrounded by an audience of well-wishers. Thank you one and all.

* * *

This book is dedicated to all those persons that wish to improve themselves and through that growth attain the abundant riches the Kingdom of God offers. May this work aid you in your journey.

CONTENTS

BOOK 3

BOOK 4

INTRODUCTION

"Two roads diverged in a yellow wood, …". This opening line from Robert Frost's poem "The Road Not Taken,"[1] serves as an appropriate beginning to this manifesto because we too stand at the gateway of two divergent roads. There is one, the one the authors believe we are currently on, where we are making tremendous progress in a plethora of areas. It would be hard to say that this path is wrong or bad if by itself considered. However, there is a cost to such progress. How does progress for progress's sake impact humanity? We are seeing a drifting away for people's consideration of those around us, far and wide and especially up close and personal.

The second path, the one which this manifesto hopes to instill in society is more about recapturing personal responsibility and community wholeness. Where putting others first for the sake of the greater community is foremost.

The difference for us will be in the decision we too make; do we take the path travelled by most of society today? Or do we take the one less travelled?

* * *

This manuscript is meant to be a guide for those wishing to attain the highest level of their potential possible. If we are to advance as a species we must evolve into a more benevolent organism. The rampant focus on self is inherently destructive. No great society exists, or ever has, that put the individual above the community. In today's world, community spans all societies. We have come to depend on each other in a way never before seen. It will serve us well to embrace this philosophy. At its core are the ideals of self-sacrifice, personal responsibility, and mutually assured assistance.

*   *   *

This manuscript basically consists of four sections called books. Each book covers a specific aspect of the philosophy. The first book deals with the core principles on which the philosophy relies. There are thirteen, divided into triads addressing common themes. Each triad is preceded by a brief introduction totaling four introductions. Principal thirteen has no introduction but rather serves as a summation of the end result.

The second book looks at the eight roles that the philosophy deals with. The book as a whole has a brief introduction followed by the roles themselves.

The third book formulates the purpose and accompanying action plan that the philosophy hopes to address. It consists of an introduction followed by two specific chapters.

Finally, book four puts forth the vision that articulates what the founders of The Charlois Philosophy have faith will occur as a result of instituting this philosophy as a movement.

*   *   *

As you read this Manifesto the question may arise, "Have the authors forsaken their Judeo-Christian roots?" We do not believe so. What we have tried to do is to more fully embrace the Christian movement of the early church. In those early years, 1st century and following, it appears the church was more inclusive than we see later, even up to and including the present age.

During Jesus's ministry we read where He told the disciples, "If they not be against us then they're for us, leave them be." (Mark 9:40 NRSV) Then in Acts we read where Peter has a vision and hears God saying, "do not call unclean that which I have made clean." (Acts 10:15 NRSV) Finally, Paul writes, "there is neither Jew or Gentile, slave or free, male or female, for we are all one in Christ Jesus." (Galatians 3:28 NRSV)

In this document we have tried to explore the teachings that all faith traditions share at their core, Love God, neighbor, and self. It is through these common teachings that we find unity as all of God's children. Working together to bring about His Kingdom on Earth.

We will acknowledge the fact that some of these teachings are at the fringes of what is orthodox but we have found that in various times and places all the precepts of the Charlois Life have been accepted and taught.

It is our hope that even if you disagree with some aspect of this Philosophy, you don't ignore all of it but rather use what you find beneficial and give grace on the rest.

BOOK 1

INTRODUCTION
1ˢᵀ TRIAD OF PRINCIPALS

Matthew 22:34-40 "…You shall love the Lord your God with all your heart, and with all your soul, and with all your mind. …. you shall love your neighbor as yourself." (Matthew 22:34-40 NRSV)

When He quoted this passage, He was responding to a question from a Pharisee, a lawyer, who was asking for the core of the law. We use it here because, like then, these pieces of the law are the core of the Charlois Philosophy. These first three principles are in their own way giving meaning to love God, love neighbor, and love self.

Principle one summarizes who God, creation, and the universe is. In its totality, it is where it all begins, and as we'll see when we get to principle thirteen, where it ends. "I am the Alpha and Omega, the beginning and the end." (Revelation 22:13 NRSV)[2]

Principle two is a moral code that details how we are to love neighbor. While being unique to this philosophy, it does draw on many of the moral codes from throughout history.

Principle three is a guide as to what loving self might look like. Although not binding, it does outline practices that benefit the individual.

As we said, these first three principles form the core of what this philosophy hopes to embody.

CHAPTER 1

PRINCIPLE #1

"The Universe consists of God and All His Creation, and functions as an interrelated whole."

"In the beginning when God created the heavens and the earth…"[3] (Genesis 1:1, NRSV)

This is the first verse of the epic poem of creation from the Judeo-Christian tradition. In it is recorded a beautiful story of how everything came into being and who caused it to occur. It establishes God as creator and as such sovereign of it all.

In another scenario, the scientific community believes that some billions of years ago there was a giant explosion and the universe came into being in a "big bang," evolving and growing ever since.

Deists believe that whatever scenario one chooses to believe the evidence reasonably points to the assumption that there must be a master architect which we call God. This manifesto does not try to prove or disprove either of the first two scenarios. However, using reason we will be moving forward on the premise that there is an intelligence behind it all and as creator this conscious being is entitled to our reverence.

For an intelligence to be able to create all that we see and know this being must be omniscient, omnipotent, and omnipresent. This being true we would think that said creator would be unknowable, but in reality, we can know, at least in part, this creator.

Very simply, the God of the universe is one being in three parts: Father, Son, and Holy Spirit. As Father, He is a conscious being that encompasses the whole of creation. He has personality as well as thought and substance; a totality of being.

As Son, we are speaking of one of the manifestations of this being, the physical part. In essence all matter, in whatever form comprises this manifestation. Whether it be the simplest atom, or the most advanced organism. All substance is in and a part of the whole being of God.

The Holy Spirit on the other hand is made up of that which we cannot see. The life force or thought of God. All matter has a vibration to it producing a frequency of energy. It is this energy that is the substance of the Holy Spirit. And as such, it too is a piece of the totality of God.

These three components of God working together is what created the universe that we know. The consciousness or Father, the physical or son, and the energy or Holy spirit, working as an interrelated whole to bring about creation or all that we see and know.

* * *

God is the creator of the universe but there is also the creation. "Created in the image of God") (Genesis 1:26 NRSV) it also has three parts: Consciousness or individuality, physical or body, and life force or spirit.

The first part, consciousness, is the individuality of the whole. It is what makes us unique, a part of God yet separate and distinct. It is believed by some that all matter possesses this consciousness to some extent. This means that all matter, be it the simplest element or the most advanced life form, has at its core a level of being, which makes us related at the individual level. However, for our purposes we shall concentrate on humankind.

The next part, physical, is the visible matter that makes up the universe. In regards to humankind, it is our bodies, comprised of various particles and elements, working together to make a living organism. Without the synergy of its various parts the body would just be dust. Yet, by working together, the pieces are able to bring about a level of being that does not exist in most of the other physical parts of the universe such as rocks, minerals, and such; again, making us unique.

The final part, spirit, is where God mostly resides in us. It has been said that the Spirit of God or the mind of God is where we have our basic connection with the divine. It is where our life and thought originates, and also where we connect with the universal spirit of the whole of creation. It is through this connection that our greatest potential comes from. In fact, working synergistically, all parts of creation, we believe can bring to fruition God's ultimate plan, heaven on Earth.

*   *   *

Finally, there is the interconnectedness of all things. God is the creator, and creation / everything else, is His handiwork. Creation is infused with God's presence, sharing a physical and spiritual aspect. However, they are separate and distinct, each with their own individual consciousness, thus connected but never one.

It is through this interconnectedness that the synergy comes about. Looking at it as a living organism, creation has many parts, all distinct and separate, but combining in common, things happen that would not be possible if the universe consisted of one type of element. Thus, it is the interaction between the parts that makes it all possible. God, the creator, working through creation, constructs His ultimate plan.

CHAPTER 2

PRINCIPLE #2

"The presence of a comprehensive Moral Code helps to assure an ordered society."

"Then God spoke all these words…" "Exodus 20:1 NRSV)

These words from the Judeo-Christian Scriptures begin, what occurs in many societies, a pronouncement from God of the moral code He desires to govern human interaction. We do not claim such an event, however we do believe that this code is divinely inspired.

Looking through many of these codes from history it becomes apparent that they are written in the negative. It becomes "Thou shalt not…" whatever it is expected we abstain from. This may control the population to a certain extent however it has been said, "the only way for evil to flourish is for good people to do nothing." With that idea in mind, we believe it would be better to inspire the population to do good than to control them by limiting their behavior. ergo, it is with that guidance that the following ten items are written in positive language.

*　　*　　*

The code which follows comes from a selection of codes from many societies. While not exhaustive it does include enough to make it inspirational in nature.

1) Practice mutual respect.

Mutual respect is the foundation upon which great relationships are built. By practicing respect, the underlying fear that each other might be taken advantage of is removed thus allowing for growth of a synergistic relationship.

2)Practice life giving habits.

Most moral codes have the provision of do no harm or thou shall not kill. While these account for some stability within a society, they do not necessarily bring about good will. Whereas do good to others builds in an atmosphere of reciprocity, with both parties trying to supersede the other in kindness.

3) Practice compassionate honesty.

Being honest is crucial if a society is to flourish, however, pure honesty can be harmful in some instances. By adding compassion to our honesty has the ability to say the truth in a loving manner.

4) Practice respect for others property.

When we practice respect for others property, we care for it as if it is our own without taking away the value of ownership held by our peers. When this is done an attitude of sharing arises, benefiting everyone.

5) Practice appropriate intimate relationships.

Intimacy is one of those practices that can bring a deeper, more loving relationship, but it needs to be practiced in appropriate settings where there is already a growing bond. To do otherwise has the potential to bring about harm, even if unintentional.

6) Practice charity

The act of giving of one's self and possessions in a sacrificial manner sends the message, "you are valued." This is something that many need to hear. We sometimes fall prey to bad times and we feel no one cares. Charity quashes that or at least lessens the blow.

7) Practice simplicity.

By practicing the simple life, a person removes greed from the equation of life. By living within ones means a whole world of contentment opens up bringing about happiness.

8 Practice justice.

The need for justice in our world is paramount. Without justice our societies collapse and we become a people believing an eye for an eye, and a tooth for a tooth no longer satisfies the urge for revenge.

9) Practice mercy.

Seek mercy in all encounters because without it anger takes the upper hand. Do unto others has us seeking a more loving way of being in relationship.

10) Practice humility.

With humility a person no longer is driven to outdo others. It is taking appropriate pride in one's accomplishments without thinking too highly of self.

These 10 when practiced faithfully will go to great lengths in alleviating the evil in the World and fostering good will among all peoples.

CHAPTER 3

PRINCIPLE #3

Success in attaining a desired future is facilitated with a system of self-discipline practices.

"Determine never to be idle. No person will have occasion to complain of the want of time who never loses any. It is wonderful how much may be done if we are always doing." (Thomas Jefferson.)

Thomas Jefferson was one of many polymaths and serves as one example of what can be accomplished with a well-disciplined life. Like most polymaths, Mr. Jefferson found the time, a discipline to be exercised, to study and practice a wide variety of interests. It was his disciplines that made him one of the greats of history.

It is through embracing a disciplined life that a person can become the best version of themselves. By emulating the greats of history and striving to reach our full potential, we too may attain greatness. At the very minimum it enables us to make a positive contribution to society.

There is no way to receive that which we desire than to practice the habits that are laid out in this principle. They are personal but at the same time affect how we relate to the world around us; the structures, relationships, and practices are all impacted by the way these habits are or are not carried out in our lives.

1) Silence

The first discipline we need to develop is silence. For it is in the act of silence that we can most clearly hear that which is most important.

2) Temperance

Temperance is the art of partaking of everything in moderation. Not overindulging in life permits us the opportunity to truly savor the riches of God's bounty.

3) Tranquility

Living free from disturbances in a state of calm assurance we can reduce our natural stress experiences. We can face everything knowing that we are in control.

4)Frugality

Frugality rewards us by always having enough. Proper care in handling our resources benefits us beyond measure. Eliminating the temptation to indulge in frivolous pursuits.

5) Order

Out of order comes efficiency. By having routines and systems in place that control the standards of our lives eliminates wasted time. By not needing to recreate every instance we can spend more time on the important items.

6) Industry

We enjoy the fruits of our labor more when we practice working hard to accomplish a goal. That which comes the hardest is often times appreciated the most.

7) Cleanliness

Cleanliness goes a long way to presenting a good image and therefore our character is strengthened. It also sharpens one's eye for detail, a skill that is valuable in all walks of life.

8) Austerity

By living the uncluttered life of austerity, we can be most focused on the things of lasting value in our lives. By limiting the frivolous things in our lives, we are making room for that which gives meaning.

9) Study

Study is crucial if we are to continue learning our whole lives. Learning our whole lives is one of the keys to becoming the best we can be. By being at our best we are more likely to accomplish great things.

10) Self Reflection

At the end of the day if we are to look back and reflect, we can possibly find places where we got it right. At the same time our mistakes can be seen and corrected. Both necessary for our personal growth.

By practicing these habits, we are endowed with the characteristics necessary to accomplish anything we set our minds to. This is part of our quest; being the best we can be so we can aid others in their quest.

INTRODUCTION
2ND TRIAD OF PRINCIPALS

The "Yoga Sutras" serves as a backdrop for this 2nd Triad of Principles. This document has been the cornerstone of "Classical Yoga" for generations. It covers the eight limbs of Raja Yoga, some of which will be used for this second set of Principals.

These limbs go something like this; the first two, moral discipline and self-discipline, were touched on in the first triad. The next three, that finish out the outer limbs are: posture, breath control, and sensory inhibition, are used in a modified format.

We take breath control first as a way to access the spiritual realm where our life force comes from. Next is posture or rather the physical practices. These are meant to ready ourselves for the job of being the temple of God. Finally, is sensory inhibition. Actually, we modify it from cancelling out the senses to enhancing them so that we can enjoy them as the gift of God they are meant to be.

In a sense, this second triad is all about preparing ourselves: spirit, body, and soul, to experience the kingdom of God.

CHAPTER 4

PRINCIPLE #4

We are first of all Spiritual Beings that need to nurture our connection with the Greater Spiritual presence of God.

"Then the Lord God formed man from the dust of the ground, and breathed into his nostrils the breath of life; and the man became a living being." (Genesis 2:7 NRSV)

God first created the physical man but we did not become living beings until He breathed the breath of life into us. It is through this life force, the Spirit of God, that we complete our being made in the image of God.

Various traditions speak of this spirit in differing ways. But for all of them it is an energy that permeates all of creation. As was mentioned earlier, all matter vibrates, creating a frequency of energy that animates the substance. To cut off this vibration would be the end of life.

Nurturing this spirit is necessary if we are to continue being living beings. Without the life force that God provides we are a mere collection of elemental atoms. By caring for our spiritual selves, we are assuring ourselves of the benefits and power of being connected to the Creator.

We nurture this connection by participating in various spiritual disciplines. Some of these, although not exhaustive, are as follows...

1) Prayer

Prayer is where we converse with our creator. There is no single set way of doing it, it can be as formal as written prayers recited as in a worship service, or as simple as a friendly conversation with one's closest friend. These prayers don't even have to be spoken, because God hears the intentions and groanings of the heart.

2) Meditation

Whereas prayer is speaking with God, meditation is where we are listening to and experiencing Him. There are many ways in which to meditate, but they all consist in focusing on God through some medium. In this way we use our senses to experience His voice or presence.

3) Study

This is where we learn about God and His ways. For many traditions it is recommended that this study focus on the scriptures or sacred readings of the faith. With the Charlois Philosophy we take a broader view. It is felt that God speaks and can be known through any and all expressions. It is because of this that we hold as scripture any expression that speaks God's love in whatever form.

4) Fasting

Taken in its most basic manifestation fasting is the act of sacrificial denial of something for the purpose of developing a deeper relationship with the Father.

5) Breath control

It has long been understood that by controlling one's breath we can affect physiological changes. This is thought to result from its spiritual connections. We may calm or excite ourselves merely by changing the rate and duration of our breaths thus opening ourselves to an influx of the life-giving aspects of the spirit.

These five disciplines form the basis of the spiritual practices used by most faith traditions. There are others, that while beneficial are not as widely experienced or understood. These esoteric practices are of value to those who understand and appreciate them.

It is because of misunderstandings that they are demonized in some circles. However, when we study them in more detail, we come to realize that they are just an alternative way of connecting with and worshipping the Creator and Sustainer of all of creation.

While we may not choose to practice or even believe in any or all of them, each and every one has been used by people through the ages to value and so we should not criticize their use because we don't understand them. Whatever method we use to connect with God, without turning it into an object of our worship, is valuable in our search for that Spiritual connection.

CHAPTER 5

PRINCIPLE #5

We are physical beings that house the Spirit and as such we should care for it as the Temple of God.

"Do you not know that you are God's temple and that God's Spirit dwells in you?" (1 Corinthians 3:16 NRSV)

As spiritual beings we have life, but where does that life reside? Our physical bodies: flesh and bone, organs and systems come together in one place. For the most efficient functioning of this body, it must be in a state of well-being.

The body of a human being is a miraculous work. This body of ours is designed in such a way that through proper care and development it theoretically could last forever and could give years of productive service.

The problem is we do not maintain it the way we need to. There are all sorts of outside factors that can wreak havoc on its resilience. But when we take the proper steps, this organism is quite remarkable in what it can endure.

Therefore, as physical beings it is of the utmost importance that we care for ourselves in a thorough and thought-out manner. Paying attention to details of recovery and development can go a long way in getting the greatest benefit out of this structure.

Human beings are notorious about using their tools and not caring for them appropriately. This not only diminishes the potential we are created with but also shortens the shelf life of effective use.

A complete program of care would include 7 areas of care as follows...

1) Rest

Rest is necessary because the body needs quality time to recover and repair from the stress placed on it. The optimal amount necessary depends on the individual, however, a good rule of thumb would be between 7-9 hours nightly.

2) Nutrition - what we put into our bodies affects many areas and so we should choose with caution.

3) Aerobic - our cardio-pulmonary systems provide the oxygen and other elements crucial to our function. Therefore, a structured program strengthening those systems is imperative.

4) Strength - our muscular/skeletal systems need to be challenged on a consistent basis to provide the functioning necessary to live a full and productive life.

5) Flexibility - Our joints and connective tissues deteriorate over time and therefore need to be stretched and flexed frequently to maintain their elasticity.

6) Balance - A host of systems work together to provide us with stability and spatial awareness needed to get through life. If we fail to practice our balance regularly, we soon become limited in what we may attempt.

7) Cleansing - With all that our bodies go through we build up a tremendous amount of toxins and other waste products. Therefore, extreme care must be taken to assure we are properly cleansing our systems of these poisons.

By following a comprehensive program of self-care, we can be assured that we will be able to perform the way we were designed for many years.

CHAPTER 6

PRINCIPLE #6

We are sentient beings that can best partake of the magnificence of creation by refining our seven senses.

"{Leonardo reflected that the average human] Looks without seeing, listens without hearing, touches without feeling, eats without tasting, moves without physical awareness, inhales without awareness of odor or fragrance, and talks without thinking." (From, "How To Think Like Leonardo Da Vinci, by Michael Gelb")

The senses are the keys to opening the doors to human experience. With the vast array of things to experience, it would be a shame to let our senses so deteriorate that we miss the pleasures they bring.

In Raja Yoga, the fifth practice is, according to the Yoga Sutras, the act of sensory inhibition. This in no way is meant to infer that the senses are wrong and feelings bad; actually, it is preparation for the higher reaches of Yoga. In fact, in some meditative practices, the act of canceling out most feeling is crucial to experiencing the focus of meditation in its fullest.

It should be noted that the act of over-indulging the senses goes contrary to most faith traditions. However, the act of refining the senses, not to indulge, but to more fully appreciate the gifts God has so freely given makes perfect sense.

We have been created with various gifts and characteristics which enable us to experience the universe around us. The first of these are...

1) Sight

2) Hearing

3) Smell

4) Taste

5) Touch

These five constitute what is commonly believed to be the way sentient beings experience the world. Because of that we feel it would be unnecessary to elaborate here. The last two are what we would call extrasensory.

6) Intuition

That extra sense that we sometimes speak of when we say things like, "I feel it in my gut," or "I just know." It is the sense that is difficult to explain. However, research shows it does exist and can be developed to our benefit.

7) Emotion

Peace, joy, happiness, anger, sadness, and the list goes on, these are the extras that move us more so than the basic five that begin our list.

By refining these senses, developing them to their full capacity, we enhance our ability to experience life. Since all of life is a gift from God, we believe that enhancing the experience of living it to its fullest extent helps us to draw closer to Him from which we come.

All of these gifts are malleable which suggests that we should strive to malleate them as possible.

INTRODUCTION
3RD TRIAD OF PRINCIPALS

Stephen Covey wrote a book called the "7 Habits of Highly Effective People." This book which we use as a basis for the 3rd Triad of Principals, is broken down into 3 sections: Private Victory, Public Victory, and Sharpen the Saw. In it he talks of our starting out as being dependent on others. As we develop, we become more independent by working on our "Private Victories." Things such as "Personal Vision," "Personal Leadership," and "Personal Management," become our daily fare. Once we have the private victory in hand resulting in our independence we need to move on to the "Public Victory," if we are to be truly successful. This public victory consists of "Interpersonal Leadership," "Empathic Communication," and "Creative Cooperation.

The 3rd section, Sharpen the Saw is about caring for self. Since these principles are about similar foci, we will not delve into it but rather focus on our universal responsibilities.

CHAPTER 7

PRINCIPLE #7

We are individuals and as such we need to develop our independence.

"I know of no more encouraging fact than the unquestionable ability of man to elevate his life by conscious endeavor." (Henry David Thoreau)

Being independent creatures brings unique obligations and opportunities. We are the only species that we are aware of that is self-aware. As such we can impact our behavior. It was once thought that we, like other animals, were given a plan for our lives that may as well been etched in stone. Whether it was genetically, environmentally, or socially; how we behaved and functioned was beyond our control. Modern research proves that not to be the case.

Because of our ability to self-direct our individuality is even more within our ability to control. In Covey's book he calls this ability the private victory, and it has three parts. "Personal Vision, Personal leadership, and personal management," work together to enable us to be the person we desire. We can be independent from outside forces and forge the lives we want.

Personal Vision is taking control of our programming, rewriting it where necessary. By being proactive in deciding who we want to be we are taking the first step toward our independence. We look at ourselves and decide; do I want to be the way I am or would it suit me better to be more the self I envision?

Personal Leadership is the stage we come to next. We draft the map of our lives. By looking at our values, roles, and goals; and comparing that to our lives we declare we want from our vision and then plan it out. Writing a personal mission statement is a major piece of that work.

Finally, we come to personal Management. In this stage we see the plan and carry it out. Things such as scheduling, and prioritizing take on significance. It is here that the work of our lives becomes a part of our integrity, and character.

By working on these three areas, we can forge an identity to our individuality, becoming the person we believe we were created to be.

CHAPTER 8

PRINCIPLE #8

We are members of the human species and as such we need to develop our interdependence.

"Interdependence is a choice only independent people can make." (From "The 7 Habits of Highly Effective People," Stephen Covey)

We live in a very social world and it is growing more so every day. If we are to be the people we are created to be, living as fellow residents of this created universe, then we need to take these principles to heart. We cannot interact with others if we are not independent ourselves and without the synergy of working with others it is doubtful if we will ever reach our full potential as individuals and as a species.

There are three principles that go a long way in assuring we become truly interdependent. The principle of interpersonal leadership. In this area we strive to get to the appropriate solution, regardless of individual egos. When we look at everything from the mindset that the best solution rarely comes from one right position. Thinking this way opens the door to a vast array of possibilities that would not be available independently.

The principle of empathic communication teaches that to fully understand a situation it is necessary for a person to articulate the other person's position. By being able to do this we empower the dialog to take on a life of its own. That eliminates unnecessary negotiating and gets right at the situation at hand. This sets the stage for the last principle.

The principle of creative cooperation focuses on synergy, that possibility of producing more together than is possible working independently. It is an experience to behold seeing a team working in a way that generates many more options because they feed on each other's energy and ideas.

This interdependent relationship is going to be critical if we are to evolve into our potential, both as individuals and as a race of differing entities.

CHAPTER 9

PRINCIPLE 9

As members of humanity it is necessary to live responsibly and in a manner that is beneficial to God and the rest of creation.

"…Be fruitful and multiply, and fill the Earth and subdue it; and have dominion over the fish of the sea and over the birds of the air and over every living thing that moves on the Earth." (Genesis 1:26-28 NRSV)

It is in this passage from the Jewish Scriptures that we get our first example of God calling mankind to be responsible. There are countless other examples in Scripture and other places which make it clear, as the crowning achievement of God's creation, we, human beings, are to take responsibility for all of creation. As an interrelated whole we who have the capability to manage and care for the rest must exercise that capability.

It is through our acts of responsibility that it can be seen where we are interconnected. By developing our independence, we are then able to start working interdependently thus bringing about the greatest good.

This universe we live in is incomprehensible but by taking ownership in our little, individual piece we can affect the whole, allowing this organism to function in a healthy way.

The created order is set up in such a way that if we are responsible about how we live in relation to it, it becomes clear that it is self-sustaining. Therefore, by being responsible, we are assuring a perpetual existence. Care for each other, care for the planet, care for all of it because it is all we have, and that as a fragile commodity.

INTRODUCTION
4TH TRIAD OF PRINCIPALS

"The purpose of life is to discover your gift,
The work of life is to develop it,
The meaning of life is to give your gift away."
(William Shakespeare)

This quote epitomizes the course of our lives if we are to become the people we are meant to be. We are not in this world for our benefit alone but rather for that which we may contribute for the greater purpose. Therefore, discovering, developing, and then giving away our gifts is the trajectory we must follow if we are to be truly satisfied with life.

In these three chapters we discuss the reasons and process we go through in living out the mantra. At the end of our discussion, we move to principle 13 where it all comes together and we reach the promised land.

CHAPTER 10

PRINCIPAL 10

In order to maintain the proper relationship to God and creation we need to be in a state of systematic self-reflection.

Plato said it best when he quoted Socrates in Apology; "The unexamined life is a life not worth living."

(Plato, The Apology)

"Remember the past, and learn from it;
Dream about the future, and plan for it;
But never forget to live in the present,
Savoring every moment and event.

Self-examination is crucial to personal growth, and personal growth is essential if we are to become the people we were created to be.

Many philosophies promote this idea of reflection, admonishing adherents to reflect and journal. It is by practicing such discipline that we grow as individuals. Laying bare both our successes and our failures, giving us an honest appraisal of ourselves.

Once we have a view of the landscape from which we are operating, we can then mold our personal growth program on both our gifts and weaknesses, becoming the best version of ourselves possible.

CHAPTER 11

PRINCIPAL 11

Personal self-reflection is of no benefit unless we engage in a comprehensive program of continual self-improvement.

Michael Gelb wrote in his book, "How to Think Like Leonardo da Vinci", about the nearly unlimited potential of mankind and gives a 7-step process for attaining our best self. This process serves the reader as a way to become renaissance people. In an article about becoming the more academic term, polymath, an unknown author writes...

"A human being should be able to change a diaper, plan an invasion, butcher a hog, conn a ship, design a building, write a sonnet, balance accounts, build a wall, set a bone, comfort the dying, take orders, cooperate, act alone, solve equations, analyze a new problem, pitch manure, program a computer, cook a tasty meal, fight efficiently, die gallantly; specialization is for insects."

(Unknown)

In order to attain the title, "Renaissance Man" there are certain things our lives need to consist of. The first is Curiosity. We need to have an insatiable thirst for everything the universe has to offer. There are ways to feed that thirst. By becoming voracious readers, we expose ourselves to a wealth of knowledge and experience. Never before has information been so readily available. Today, with the advent of computers and the internet, we have access to most of what has been written, the ability to travel to foreign lands, and explore the cosmos in its entirety.

Second, we must be willing to test that knowledge through personal experience. Facts have a way of being distorted by people's use of them. For this reason, we must test everything so that we don't just know "stuff" but have experienced "stuff" for ourselves.

The most practical way of testing facts is through our senses. Therefore, refinement of our natural senses provides a way to get in touch with reality.

We cannot neglect the idea that our senses sometimes present conflicting information. Thus, we need to embrace ambiguity, paradox, and uncertainty. It is because of these conflicts we realize that differing ways of seeing cause us to use different parts of our reasoning faculties. Therefore...

We must develop all parts of our brains in a way that allows us to think with both logic and imagination. Using the two approaches to work on issues increases our chances of coming to resolution. Research has shown however that it is not just our brains where sensory input is processed but throughout our bodies.

Developing our whole selves is crucial to realizing our full potential. Therefore, the cultivation of grace, ambidexterity, fitness, and poise is a must for any polymath. Once we have all those pieces together it is time to work on the totality and tie it all together.

This interconnectedness of all things calls for a systems approach to dealing with life. Once we have the processes in place nothing will be beyond our reach.

CHAPTER 12

PRINCIPAL 12

Having attained that which we desire then we are best served by relinquishing control of self and all that we hold dear.

This comes from my reading of Matthew 16:3,4 where we are called to give our lives up for God, and other readings on sacrifice as well.

"Treat people with dignity, honor, and respect; esteeming them higher than yourself and they will give their lives to make you successful." (Robert A. Charlois, 2017)

Giving of oneself is the foundation on which the future society must embrace. We live in a world that like no other time in history we see the interconnectedness on a grand scale. States are more and more relying on each other for basic, and not so basic needs. The law of reciprocity served primitive civilizations well and it can the modern equally as well.

"It's not what you get from life that matters, rather, it's what you contribute that makes the difference." Robert A. Charlois

CHAPTER 13

PRINCIPAL 13

The whole purpose of living these Principles is to gain union with God and Creation in service to the highest good which is the Perfect will of God.

Revelation 21 talks of a new Heaven and a new Earth where God and man will spend eternity together.

"What must I do to inherit eternal life?"

(Mark 10:17 NRSV)

This question which has been asked in various forms since the beginning of time gets to the heart of the human quest. Man seems to be hardwired to want to seek a return to the presence of God. It's as if we are incomplete if we are not an integral part of the greater cosmos.

In man's search for meaning, it boils down to, what can I do to be a part of the greater reality? We came from God, in the beginning and to God we will return in the end.

In some faiths, there is the belief that we are recreated or born anew over and over until we evolve to a state where that return is possible.

In other traditions we are given this one life and then the judgement, where it will be determined whether we have met the criteria for eternity with God, or, eternity separated from Him.

We believe that God, given His perfect love nature, would give us every opportunity to meet whatever the criteria are. Thus, yes, we believe in some form we are given multiple chances to learn the lessons necessary to make the transition from mortal beings to that which we desire, immortality.

These principles are a way, one of many, that serves to aid us in that journey. When we follow the teachings in this manifesto, we believe we are being equipped to make that transition.

"A HEART THAT COULDN'T SLEEP LAST NIGHT."

A heart that couldn't sleep last night, for souls that anguish far below, and baptistries unused above; Would speak of things more tragic still, of hearts become as cold as stone;

When in the rush of daily things, of jobs and coin of mortal fare, why can we not more clearly see, what dangers lurk beyond the pale, and press t'ward legacies beyond, where moth and rust cannot prevail;

And on the final day we dwell, shall truth the final ledger tell, we might have done a better job, to run a race where none prevail, but in the last analysis it won't much matter where we fit, as long as we have steered our course to let our Savior settle it.

(Pastor Gordon Jones, August 10th, 2021)

BOOK 2

CHARLOIS ROLES

INTRODUCTION TO ROLES

This book focuses on the eight roles that every human possesses. They are based on the eight dimensions of wellness utilized in some mental health circles. They are: Spiritual, Physical, Intellectual, Emotional, Social, Environmental, Occupational, and Financial. While different people have various other roles: spouse, parent, etc.… these eight comprise a core that permeates all aspects of the human condition.

Being based on the eight dimensions of wellness might indicate that we are speaking of the absence of health, we are not. What we are speaking of is a balanced way of integrating our different natures into who we are. In the chapters that follow we will be looking at each role in turn and exploring how it functions alone and also in concert with the others.

By taking responsibility to develop one's self in these eight dimensions we are equipping ourselves to be the best version of what we are created to be. Failure to focus on these roles has a tendency to lead to heartache and suffering.

CHAPTER 1

SPIRITUAL ROLE

In Victor Frankl's book, "Man's search For Meaning," he talks about how man, if he has meaning and purpose in his life, can overcome any hardship. That is the role of the spiritual side of mankind. It is our spiritual nature, or "Higher Power", if you will, that gives meaning and purpose. By responsibly caring for ourselves in this role we are being enabled to have the abundant life that Frankl speaks of.

We are spiritual beings in addition to our physical manifestation and therefore we need to nurture that side of our being.

Practices such as prayer and meditation are at the base of connecting to our spiritual side but we shouldn't neglect other opportunities as well. Life is full of ways to tune in and find our core natures. Self-exploration is just as important to discovering who we are and how we relate to the universal presence.

In our spiritual role is where we connect to that presence. It is there for us and in its essence has our best interests as its purpose.

So, find your way to tapping into your higher self and realize your full potential.

CHAPTER 2

PHYSICAL ROLE

Whereas our spiritual role connects us to the universal spirit, our physical role serves to connect us with the physical aspect of creation.

In the physical role we see where our ability to function as bipeds comes in. When we get out of bed in the morning our physical systems fire up and we are able to move around. This is only possible if we take the necessary steps to ensure good health. We do this by watching our diets, getting proper exercise, monitoring our physical systems, and getting the proper care when needed.

This care is essential but the true miracle occurs when we come to understand that we are just a part of a greater whole. Engaging in physical activity we see that what we do for ourselves enables us to do for each other. This reciprocity is necessary for us to thrive as members of the universe.

If we want to be able to enjoy our lives for as long as we live, then it is essential that we take this role seriously. Otherwise, as we age our bodies will start to deteriorate robbing us of the pleasures of life.

CHAPTER 3

INTELLECTUAL ROLE

Our spiritual and physical roles are just a pair of our roles that need to be cared for. They form the foundation for the other roles such as the intellectual and emotional roles.

With the intellectual we find that research indicates that the human mind can improve with age. If this is true then we would think it to be our obligation to do all we can to aid that process. It has also been said that "a mind is a terrible thing to waste." Considering the nearly unlimited potential we have intellectually, the expansion of our capabilities should be a high priority.

Just like with our other capacities, the intellect needs to be exercised. One of the ways one does this is by offering our minds new and challenging activities. By doing this the brain forms new neural pathways to accommodate the challenge.

In addition to new activities, it is beneficial to add variability. When we learn one thing it increases our ability to understand other, totally unrelated material.

In addition to training our minds we need to care for it with proper nutrition, rest, and avoidance of toxic substances.

By providing our intellect with the proper care we are increasing our chances of being able to take advantage of opportunities the arise in other areas of our lives.

CHAPTER 4

EMOTIONAL ROLE

In our emotional role we are exposed to the variations of emotions that our senses bring about. In order to properly function we need some semblance of control over these emotions. Proper Mental Health care is a must, not only for those with a diagnosed condition but also for anyone wanting to reach their full potential.

It is not just so that we can attain our highest potential but to fully embrace the wonders of creation. Who of us have not seen the Sun rise and be moved? Nor can we contemplate the birth of a child and not be awe struck. The list could go on forever for there is no end to the emotions we experience when we encounter that which life presents.

Learning to process these emotions in a way that serves us well is where our emotional role comes in. Mis-managed, we are in danger of committing a transgression that could hamper our attempts at an awesome life.

Therefore, constant monitoring of the emotions we experience goes a long way in allowing us the life we desire.

CHAPTER 5

SOCIAL ROLE

Where would we be without the social structures that give order to our lives? Accessing the synergy that is possible when we become truly interdependent opens a universe of options. Whenever we operate in our social role, we are exponentially expanding our effectiveness.

Think about whenever we gather with family and friends, that interaction brings our Social Role into play. We are taught to act in certain ways that mimic the given social norms. Certain things we learn from an early age are taboo. Other items are up to the individual.

While this pattern serves the society well in controlling behavior, it is not the only way to survive the minefield of personalities.

We need to constantly be monitoring our interactions and make adjustments along the way. By truly listening, both to the verbal, as well as the nonverbal cues, we can ascertain that which is beneficial or not.

Practicing good social habits goes far in allowing us to function at a high level with others.

CHAPTER 6

ENVIRONMENTAL ROLE

We live in a world created to be perfect in every way, and yet, we as the caretakers of that creation have failed in our responsibilities. Instead of caring for the environment the way we should we are nearly at a place where the garden of Eden is nearly uninhabitable. In our role as caretakers, we need to take seriously our call.

Our role as environmentalists has two parts. There is our part in caring for creation; by itself, creation is self-sustaining. However, with the addition of we, as a species, there is the prevalence of taking more from the world around us than we give back. When this is carried to extremes, the world cannot care for itself and terra firma suffers. Since we are one with the rest of creation, we need to care for it as we do for ourselves.

The other aspect of these roles is that our immediate surroundings have an impact on us as a people. When our environment is cluttered or in disarray we can suffer in various ways. Proper care for our surroundings has a tremendous impact on whether we thrive or not.

Being interconnected, when we care for our environment, we are in essence caring for ourselves.

CHAPTER 7

CONTRIBUTOR ROLE

As a species we need to have a purpose in life if we are to feel fulfilled. One of our purposes is to contribute, to give back to the universe and the society we live in.

People have obligations in life, and the way to fulfilling those obligations is to be productive members of society. This is our contributory role coming into play. By engaging in some vocation where we can contribute to our fellow man and the greater society, we have found our calling.

It is not enough for us to use the resources that God provides, but in return for those blessings we need to use that which is given us to benefit others. The law of reciprocity is based on the idea that if we all contribute something then we all thrive. Those that take without giving something in return are a burden on society.

So, to fulfill this role we need to discover our gifts, the things we are good at, and find a way to use them to help others who may not be so gifted in that particular area.

CHAPTER 8

RESOURCE MANAGER ROLE

We have at our disposal an abundance of resources to be used to carry on life in this universe we live in. It is only when we fail to manage these resources appropriately that scarcity enters the equation. Therefore, it will serve us well if we learn, and carry out proper resource management principles.

Money, or the love of money is the root of all evil, the saying goes. That is why we need to take our finances seriously. Having a good respect of money without the love of it can go a long way to taking care of our financial responsibilities. Budgeting, saving, frugal living, and other aspects, go a long way in assuring that we have enough.

Human resources fall into a separate category. With money, it is not necessary to take into account how it feels about being managed; people are different and need to be considered. Developing the human relationship is therefore crucial in getting the best from those we interact with.

With our physical resources we need to be aware of ways to maintain usefulness of that which we are using. Whether it be machinery, natural resources, or property of another sort; physical items do not last forever unless cared for properly.

Proper diligence in all areas will assure our needs will be met.

BOOK 3

PURPOSE AND ACTION PLAN

INTRODUCTION TO BOOK 3

Where Book 1 laid out the principles to live by, and Book 2 gave us the Roles through which we manifest our beliefs, Book 3 will be where we make the practical application of the philosophy clear.

In this Book we will explore the purpose of the Charlois Philosophy in chapter 1, and the basic action plan for implementing the philosophy in chapters 2 through 7.

It will be in these later chapters that we will be proposing a mode of operation that, in our view best accomplishes the goal of improving people's lives. It is the plan we will be using in our life and merely serves as an example for what others may want to do.

There may be other, and possibly better ways to carry out the mission, but we present this plan as our option.

CHAPTER 1

PURPOSE

The Charlois Philosophy is intended to be a practical philosophy that serves to improve the lives of those who practice it. It incorporates a process that takes the practitioner from a self- centered being to that of one who puts others first, thus bringing everyone to a place of abundance.

Starting with an understanding of God, the universe, and the interconnectedness of all that exists, we move through different stages of development. We start with the greater whole, move through independent growth, and end up back at being united with the greater whole.

We believe that once our individual needs are met, we can then proceed to helping others in their quest for abundance. As more and more people realize their desires being met the entire creation begins to vibrate at higher frequencies. Which in turn leads to an even greater abundance of that which we seek.

"Helping improve lives, because we care," is not just a catchy slogan but rather a whole mindset behind everything Charlois.

CHAPTER 2

ACTION PLAN – PART 1

WRITTEN DOCUMENTS

The process by which the Charlois Philosophy will be carried out is that the practitioner will live the principles in each of his/her various Roles. This is true in the case of organizations as well.

The mode of operation for the combined Charlois organization will begin with this Manifesto. It is being written so as to lay down the basic understanding of what is behind the philosophy. Principles, Roles, a prototype of a possible course of action, and the vision of an abundant universe poured out for all to benefit.

Over the course of time there will be other writings that add to body of thought that is going into this life. Add to that the inclusion of a website and blog that will be discussed in a moment, and we have the foundation of what we authors envision becoming a movement that has the potential to change the world.

So, this is just a piece of the plan. A foundational document that sets in place the basics of what we are doing.

ACTION PLAN – PART 2

INTERNET PRESENCE

As mentioned in the previous section, the Charlois Philosophy will have an internet presence. This presence will serve as communication central.

There will be a basic website where an overall view of everything Charlois will be presented. Everything from the profit and nonprofit sectors to biographies and links to entities we find helpful. That means this could be your first stop to becoming acquainted with the movement.

A second aspect will be a blog. This will be the locus where we discuss the practicalities of the philosophy and keep people informed of the happenings in the movement. It will also be a great place to turn to if you are seeking to learn more than just what is in this book.

These two pieces will hopefully be adequate to handling the public relations surrounding the Charlois Life. Without a strong online presence, the movement will struggle to flourish.

With the book in hand, and information central just a click away, it's time to look at the entities that make up our proposed plan.

ACTION PLAN – PART 3

NON-PROFIT

After getting our web presence established the next item to be addressed will be the startup of a non-profit. "Fellowship Of All God's Children" will be designed to be such an entity.

Beginning as a place of fellowship, it will secure 501c(3) status at the earliest opportunity. Within this structure there will be channels directed at raising donations for its work. These donations will be disbursed as follows...

1. 50% will be designated as a fund from which grants will be made to benevolent entities for the expansion of services to those in need.
2. 40% will be designated for use by the Fellowship for the purpose of developing programs aimed at improving the lives of the members of the surrounding area.
3. Finally, 10% will be set aside for the administration of the organization.

It should be noted that according to our bylaws, no person shall receive monetary compensation from these donations.

As part of the 40% disbursement, there will be programs that address needs in all eight of the Charlois Roles. These programs will be open to all persons, regardless of any defining label. Educational classes, crusades, and other benevolent type programs will all be considered.

As required by law, "Fellowship of All God's Children," once established as a 503c1 will be guided by a board of directors. These persons will be chosen from the surrounding area. Also, their positions will be totally voluntary.

We believe that the establishment of this organization will go a long way toward improving the quality of life of those that receive assistance. This will also have as a collateral benefit, the strengthening of the community at large.

ACTION PLAN – PART 4

FOR PROFIT

All movements require some source of funding and it is for that reason, as well as others that we plan on having a for profit arm. Another reason is that there will be opportunities to impact people's lives through the businesses we envision establishing.

This arm will actually consist of a consortium of like-minded companies addressing different areas. Several will be mentioned in this document, but for this part we will focus on the one that holds center stage; Charlois General Trading.

CGT will be a retail establishment that will set itself apart by it's pricing policies. Essential items: food, health care, and sanitation items, will be marked up by half the difference between cost of goods and suggested retail, not to exceed a total of 10% markup. For non-essential items that markup shall not exceed 25%.

In addition to the low markup policies CGT will be different than most businesses in that they will donate 10% of all net profits to Fellowship of All God's Children for use in their ministries.

Another characteristic will be in that CGT, as well as all businesses in the consortium will have profit sharing for employees. 25% of net profits will go into a fund to be disbursed quarterly.

As can be seen by some of these policies, the members of the consortium have at their heart to provide their employees, customers, and communities opportunities that may not be otherwise available.

Let us now look at some of the other entities of this consortium.

ACTION PLAN – PART 5

COACHING

Another way we plan on living out this philosophy is to set up a coaching business. "Leonardo's, Bookstore and personal growth center," will provide some of the things necessary to improve life. Coaching services, personal growth resources, and training events will be linked to help people get the most out of life.

A variety of coaching programs will enable providers the opportunity to custom tailor services to specific needs and expectations. Whether it be a full, life coaching program, or individual, focused modules targeting specific areas. It will all be consumer driven.

As far as the personal growth resources, our store will be set up around the eight roles, with a section focused on products specific to each role. Then, at the heart of the store will be a book section providing quality reading items as well as packaged self-learning courses.

Finally, there will be offered on Wednesdays and Saturdays, workshops and seminars further targeting customer's needs.

Full-service life improvement center at its best.

ACTION PLAN – PART 6

THERAPEUTIC REHABILITATION

For all that a retail store and personal growth center are intended to provide, there are some who are not at a place in their lives to fully benefit from such services. In fact, assisted living and rehabilitation services are more of a match.

"The Maysville Grand," will be such a facility. For those persons that find themselves in less-than-ideal situations but still have a desire to make the most of their life, this could be the place. Regardless of physical or mental impairment, people can come here to take advantage of not only the residential accommodations but also the in / outpatient rehabilitation offerings.

Built as a multi-story structure it will include housing for overnight homeless situations as well as apartments for longer term care. There will also be a retail store, dinning facilities, classrooms, and physical therapy areas.

This will be a much-needed establishment that will take various entities to bring it into existence, but well worth it for those in need.

ACTION PLAN – PART 7

COMMUNITY

While these mentioned businesses and organizations have their place in the over-all plan of the Charlois Philosophy it reaches its full expression in "The Charlois Estate." This will be a working farm community based on the principles of Charlois.

At the heart of the community will be the residence of the chairman of the movement and its surrounding agricultural operations. Utilizing ethical farming practices, it will be self-sustaining in nature, giving back to the environment more than it takes.

Also included in the estate will be educational facilities, shopping, recreation, housing, and other businesses. It will be a self-contained community of about one square mile.

The purpose of this community will primarily be to serve as an example of what can be accomplished using this ideology, which will be taught and promoted.

With that, we have the major components of the plan for how we envision it being carried out.

CHARLOIS VISION

The vision for The Charlois Philosophy is to form a utopian society based on the Principles, Roles, and Mission as put forth in this Manifesto. This society will have no borders or other separating structures, but rather will be an all-inclusive community of persons who live their lives based on the ideals that this document details. As a society that believes in the interconnectedness of all creation, we will treat each other and creation as a whole with: dignity, honor, and respect, esteeming its inclusiveness as greater than our individuality.

"The best way to predict the future is to create it." Michael Gelb, Real Leader.

That is our hope, that we will create a world in which every person can realize their full potential and thereby be positioned to help others do the same.

"Man has not advanced much over the last 500 years. There have been advances in knowledge and technology, but mankind itself has not changed much in the last half a millennium." (Paraphrase of Kahn, Star Trek, "Space Seed" episode).

We believe that if mankind lives with the appropriate mindset, practicing the Charlois Philosophy then maybe we as a species can evolve to a higher level of organism. We further believe that this advanced entity would mature into a society that strives for continuous self-growth. By becoming the best version of ourselves we would therefore see the value of helping those we influence become the best of themselves.

EPILOGUE

We, the authors, pray that in some way this Manifesto inspires you, the reader, to practice this philosophy and are led to partake in God's new kingdom. We realize that not everyone will embrace all that is contained in its pages. No philosophy is perfect. However, we believe that by following the basic precepts, people will come to see that God, and creation form an interconnected whole. One in which God wants an eternal connection with His creation. A situation we all have access to.

So, we invite you to live the abundant life promised since the dawn of creation. Create your own version of the "Garden of Eden" and live there for eternity.

Contact the Author

If you are interested in the Charlois Philosophy you can find our website at charolaisphilosophy.com

Or

Pastoryancy611@yahoo.com

Join us and get the most out of life.

Printed in the United States
by Baker & Taylor Publisher Services